FULL COLOUR
VIEWS
OF THE
FOOTBALL LEAGUE
GROUNDS

**Photography
by
Chris Ambler**

FOREWORD

After a lifelong obsession to see all 92 Clubs in the Football League a dream has come true.

Taking just over a year and using my holidays, I managed to visit all the clubs, actually taking 16 days to do so, plus travelling 6,000 miles. 94 clubs had to be visited as Darlington were out of the league at the time plus a journey to Macclesfield now the temporary home of Chester City.

Many thanks go to all the clubs and I am indebted to the staff at the grounds for allowing me in to take the photos. Also to John Robinson and Roy Adlard without whom this book would not have been possible.

Chris Ambler

British Library Cataloguing in Publication Data
1. U.K. Association Football
   Football League Grounds
AMBLER, CHRIS 1945-
796.334.66
ISBN 0-947808-14-0

© CHRIS AMBLER and SOCCER BOOK PUBLISHING LTD. 1990
   Published in Great Britain by
   Soccer Book Publishing Limited
   72 St. Peters Avenue
   CLEETHORPES, DN35 8HU

Set in Century 10/11
Printed in Great Britain by
ADLARD PRINT & TYPESETTING SERVICES, RUDDINGTON, NOTTINGHAM

View from the East Bank Terrace

Looking from the High Street End

View from the North Bank

Looking from the South Terrace

View from the North Stand

Looking from the Holte End

View from the Spion Kop

Looking from the Pontefract Road End

View from the Tilton Road End

Looking from the Cattell Road Stand

View from the end of the Riverside Stand

8

Looking from the Kidder Street End

View from the South Stand

Looking from the Spion Kop

View from the end of the Great Lever Stand

Looking from Embankment

View from the South Stand

Looking from the Brighton Beach Terrace

View from Main Stand

Looking from the Spion Kop

View from Main Stand

Looking from Brook Road End

View from the N.E. Terrace

Looking from the South Stand

View from the Covered End

Looking from the Ashton Road End

View from the Bristol End

Looking from the Bath End

View from the Bee Hole Lane End

Looking from the Cricket Field Stand

View from the Manchester Road End

Looking from the Cemetery End

View from the Allotment End

Looking from the North Stand

View from the Grangetown End

Looking from the Canton Stand

View from the Warwick Road End

Looking from the Main Stand

View from Whitehorse Lane End

Looking from Holmesdale Road End

View from the South Terrace

Looking from the North Terrace

View from the Town End

Looking towards 'The Bramble' Hotel

View from the Cross Street End

Looking from the Saltergate End

View from the end of the Swan Lane Terrace

Looking from the West Stand

View from the Railway End

Looking from the Gresty Road End

View from the Members Terrace

Looking from the end of the Main Stand

View from the Cricket Ground End

Looking from the South End

View from the Osmaston Stand

Looking from the Vulcan Street End

View from the Rossington End

Looking from the Town End

View from Gwladys Street Stand

Looking from Park End Terrace

View from the Big Bank

Looking from the St. James Road End

View from the Putney End

Looking from the Hammersmith End

View from the Priestfield Road End

Looking from the Rainham End

View from the Pontoon Stand End

Looking from the Osmond Stand

View from the Open Terrace End

Looking from the Hunger Hill End

View from the Rink End

Looking from the Town End

View from Merton Meadow End

Looking from Blackfriars Street End

View from the Dalton Bank End

Looking from the Leeds Road End

View from the South Stand

Looking from the North Terrace

View from the South Stand

Looking from the Portman Stand

View from the Elland Road End

Looking from the North Stand End

View from South Stand

Looking from North Stand

View from the North Terrace

Looking from the South Terrace

View from the new Railway Stand

Looking towards the City End

View from the Main Stand

Looking from the Kop

View from the Kenilworth Road End

Looking from the Oak Road Stand

View from the Watling Street End

Looking from the North End

View from the end of the Main Stand

Looking from the end of the Kippax Stand

View from the Family Stand

Looking from the Stretford End

View from the Quarry Lane End

Looking from the North Stand

View from the East End

Looking from the Holgate End

View from Ilderton Road End

Looking from Cold Blow Lane End

View from the Gallowgate End

Looking from the Leazes End

View from the Spion Kop

Looking from the Hotel End

View from the River End Stand

Looking from the Barclay Stand

View from the Colwick Road End

Looking from the Trent End

View from the Spion Kop

Looking from the Meadow Lane End

View from the Rochdale Road End

Looking from the Chadderton Stand

View from the Osler Road side

Looking from the London Road End

View from the Glebe Road Terrace

Looking from the Moys End

View from the Peverell End

Looking from the Devonport End

View from the Milton End

Looking from the Fratton End

View from the Hamil Road End

Looking from Bycars Road End

View from the Fulwood End

Looking from the Town End

View from the West End Stand

Looking from the Loftus Road Stand

View from the Tilehurst End

Looking from the Suffolk Road End

View from the Pearl Street End

Looking from the Sandy Lane Stand

View from the Railway End

Looking from the Tivoli End

View from the Seamer Road End

Looking from the Edgehill Road End

View from the South Stand

Looking from the Red Mill Terrace

View from the end of the Bramall Lane Stand

73

Looking from the corner of the Main Stand and Spion Kop

View from the corner of the West Stand

Looking from the Spion Kop

View from the Station End

Looking from the Milton Road End

View from the Milton Road End

Looking from the Archers Road End

View from the North Bank

Looking from the South Bank

View from the Railway End

Looking from the Cheadle End

View from the Boothen End

Looking from the Stoke End

View from the Roker End

Looking from the Fulwell End

View from the East Stand

Looking from the West Terrace

View from the Stratton Bank

Looking from the Town End

View from the Popular Side

Looking from the Warbro Road End

View from the North Stand

Looking from the Park Lane End

View from the Bebington Kop End

Looking from the Town End

View from the Main Stand

Looking from the South Stand

View from the Rous Stand

Looking from the Vicarage Road End

View from the Smethwick End

Looking from the Birmingham Road End

View from the North Bank

Looking from the Castle Street End

View from the Town End

Looking from the Shevington End

View from the Wandle End

Looking from the South Stand

View from the John Ireland Stand

Looking from the South Bank

View from the Town End

Looking from the Border Stand

View from the Bootham Crescent End

Looking from the Shipton Street End

ALDERSHOT FC

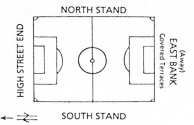

NORTH STAND
HIGH STREET END
EAST BANK (Away) Covered Terraces
SOUTH STAND

ASTON VILLA FC

TRINITY ROAD STAND & ENCLOSURE
Holte End
NORTH STAND (MEMBERS ONLY) WITTON END TERRACE (AWAY – COVERED)
(Home)   (Away)
WITTON LANE STAND
BUS

BIRMINGHAM CITY FC

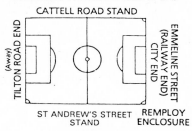

CATTELL ROAD STAND
(Away) TILTON ROAD END
EMMELINE STREET (RAILWAY END) CITY END
ST ANDREW'S STREET STAND
REMPLOY ENCLOSURE

BLACKPOOL FC

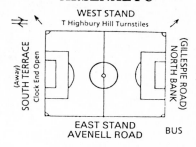

BUS
WEST STAND
SPION KOP : EAST SECTION
BLOOMFIELD ROAD SOUTH STAND
(Away) EAST SECTION
(Away)
EAST PADDOCK: NORTH SECTION
HENRY STREET

AFC BOURNEMOUTH

THISTLE BARROW RD. NEW STAND
KINGS PARK CAR PARK SOUTH STAND
BRIGHTON BEACH TERRACE (Away)
MAIN STAND CAR PARK
('A' BLOCK) INVALID ENTRANCE

ARSENAL FC

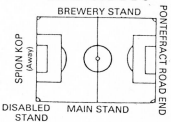

WEST STAND
T Highbury Hill Turnstiles
(Away) SOUTH TERRACE Clock End Open
(GILLESPIE ROAD) NORTH BANK
EAST STAND AVENELL ROAD
BUS

BARNSLEY FC

BREWERY STAND
SPION KOP (Away)
PONTEFRACT ROAD END
DISABLED STAND
MAIN STAND

BLACKBURN ROVERS FC

RIVERSIDE LANE WALKERSTEEL STAND
KIDDER STREET BLACKBURN END
DARWEN END (Away)
NUTTALL STREET STAND BOLTON ROAD

BOLTON WANDERERS FC

BURNDEN STAND
EMBANKMENT (Away)
GREAT LEVER STAND
BUS   MANCHESTER ROAD STAND

BRADFORD CITY FC

T & A MIDLAND ROAD FAMILY STAND
SPION KOP
HOLLYWELL ASH LANE (Away)
NATPRO'S STAND

BRENTFORD FC

NEW ROAD STAND

BROOK ROAD END

EALING ROAD END (Away)

(CLOCK END)

MAIN STAND
BRAEMAR ROAD

BRISTOL CITY FC

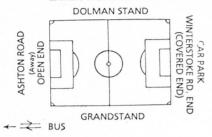

DOLMAN STAND

ASHTON ROAD (Away) OPEN END

WINTERSTOKE RD. END (COVERED END)
CAR PARK

GRANDSTAND

BUS

BURNLEY FC

(Away)
COVERED TERRACING

BELVEDERE ROAD
HANSON STAND

BEE HOLE LANE

BOB LORD STAND
BRUNSHAW ROAD

BUS

CAMBRIDGE UNITED FC

ELFLEDA ROAD
MAIN STAND

NEWMARKET ROAD
NORTH STAND

ALLOTMENT END (Away)

HABBIN STAND

T Visitors
Entrance

CARLISLE UNITED FC

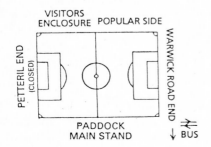

VISITORS
ENCLOSURE   POPULAR SIDE

PETTERIL END (CLOSED)

WARWICK ROAD END

PADDOCK
MAIN STAND

BUS

BRIGHTON & HOVE ALBION FC

GOLDSTONE LANE
(Away)
N.E. TERRACE EAST TERRACE

OLD SHOREHAM RD.
NORTH TERRACE

NEWTOWN ROAD
SOUTH STAND

WEST STAND
NEWTOWN ROAD

BRISTOL ROVERS FC

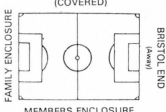

HOME ENCLOSURE
(COVERED)

FAMILY ENCLOSURE

BRISTOL END (Away)

MEMBERS ENCLOSURE
MAIN STAND

BURY FC

BUS

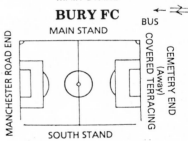

MAIN STAND

MANCHESTER ROAD END

CEMETERY END (Away)
COVERED TERRACING

SOUTH STAND

CARDIFF CITY FC

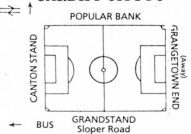

POPULAR BANK

CANTON STAND

GRANGETOWN END (Away)

BUS

GRANDSTAND
Sloper Road

CHARLTON ATHLETIC FC

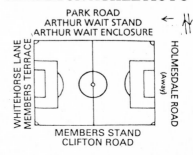

PARK ROAD
ARTHUR WAIT STAND
ARTHUR WAIT ENCLOSURE

WHITEHORSE LANE
MEMBERS TERRACE

HOLMESDALE ROAD (Away)

MEMBERS STAND
CLIFTON ROAD

CHELSEA FC

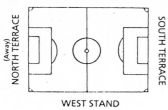

EAST STAND

(Away) NORTH TERRACE

SOUTH TERRACE

WEST STAND

CHESTERFIELD FC

COMPTON STREET SIDE

SALTERGATE SPION KOP

CROSS STREET END (Away)

MAIN STAND
ST. MARGARET'S DRIVE

CREWE ALEXANDRA FC

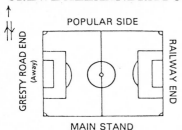

POPULAR SIDE

GRESTY ROAD END (Away)

RAILWAY END

MAIN STAND

DARLINGTON FC

WEST STAND (Away)

FEETHAMS CRICKET GROUND VICTORIA ROAD

POLAM LAND SOUTH END

EAST STAND
RIVER SKERNE

DONCASTER ROVERS FC

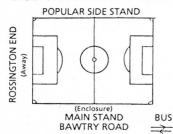

POPULAR SIDE STAND

ROSSINGTON END (Away)

(Enclosure)
MAIN STAND
BAWTRY ROAD   BUS

CHESTER CITY FC

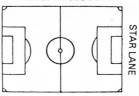

FAMILY ENCLOSURE

STAR LANE

COVENTRY CITY FC

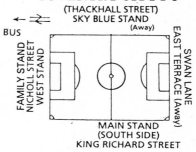

(THACKHALL STREET)
SKY BLUE STAND
(Away)

BUS

FAMILY STAND NICHOLL STREET WEST STAND

SWAN LANE EAST TERRACE (Away)

MAIN STAND
(SOUTH SIDE)
KING RICHARD STREET

CRYSTAL PALACE FC

PARK ROAD
ARTHUR WAIT STAND
ARTHUR WAIT ENCLOSURE

WHITEHORSE LANE MEMBERS TERRACE

HOLMESDALE ROAD (Away)

MEMBERS STAND
CLIFTON ROAD

DERBY COUNTY FC

(Away)   (Home)
CO-OP STAND

OSMASTON STANDS (Away)

VULCAN STREET NORMANTON STANDS

SHAFTESBURY CRESCENT

EVERTON FC

BULLENS ROAD

GWLADYS STREET STAND

GOODISON AVENUE PARK END TERRACING (Away)

BUS   GOODISON ROAD
MAIN STAND

97

EXETER CITY FC

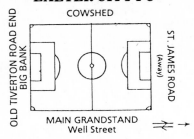

COWSHED

OLD TIVERTON ROAD END
BIG BANK

ST. JAMES ROAD
(Away)

MAIN GRANDSTAND
Well Street

GILLINGHAM FC

GORDON ROAD STAND

TORONTO ROAD
RAINHAM END

GILLINGHAM END
Priestfield Road

MAIN STAND
Redfern Avenue

HALIFAX TOWN FC

Huddersfield Road (A629)
MAIN STAND

OPEN TERRACE
(Away)

HUNGER HILL

FAMILY &
DISABLED STAND

HEREFORD UNITED FC

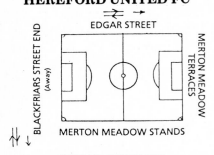

EDGAR STREET

BLACKFRIARS STREET END
(Away)

MERTON MEADOW
TERRACES

MERTON MEADOW STANDS

HULL CITY FC

EAST STAND

BOOTHFERRY ROAD
NORTH TERRACE
(Away)

SOUTH STAND

MAIN STAND
NORTH ROAD

FULHAM FC

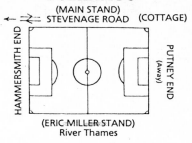

(MAIN STAND)
STEVENAGE ROAD   (COTTAGE)

HAMMERSMITH END

PUTNEY END
(Away)

(ERIC MILLER STAND)
River Thames

GRIMSBY TOWN FC

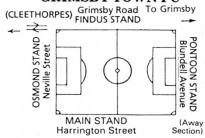

(CLEETHORPES) Grimsby Road To Grimsby
FINDUS STAND

OSMOND STAND
Neville Street

PONTOON STAND
Blundell Avenue

MAIN STAND
Harrington Street

(Away
Section)

HARTLEPOOL UNITED FC

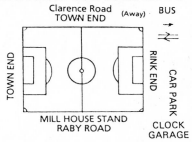

Clarence Road   (Away)   BUS
TOWN END

TOWN END

RINK END

CAR PARK

MILL HOUSE STAND
RABY ROAD

CLOCK
GARAGE

HUDDERSFIELD TOWN FC

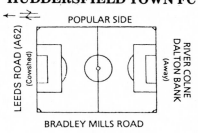

POPULAR SIDE

LEEDS ROAD (A62)
(Cowshed)

RIVER COLNE
DALTON BANK
(Away)

BRADLEY MILLS ROAD

IPSWICH TOWN FC

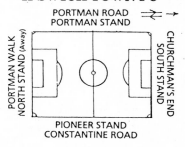

PORTMAN ROAD
PORTMAN STAND

PORTMAN WALK
NORTH STAND (Away)

CHURCHMAN'S END
SOUTH STAND

PIONEER STAND
CONSTANTINE ROAD

LEEDS UNITED FC

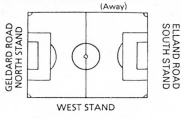

LOWFIELD ROAD STAND
(Away)

GELDARD ROAD NORTH STAND

ELLAND ROAD SOUTH STAND

WEST STAND

LEYTON ORIENT FC

OLIVER ROAD WEST STAND

BUCKINGHAM ROAD SOUTH TERRACE (Away)

WINDSOR ROAD NORTH TERRACE

MAIN STAND BRISBANE ROAD

LIVERPOOL FC

Visitors Section

KEMLYN ROAD STAND

ANFIELD ROAD

WALTON BRECK ROAD SPION KOP

PADDOCK ENCLOSURE MAIN STAND LOTHAIR ROAD

MAIDSTONE UNITED FC

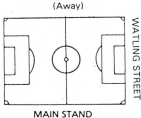

ST. JOHN'S ROAD (Away)

WATLING STREET

MAIN STAND

MANCHESTER UNITED FC

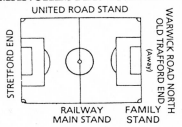

UNITED ROAD STAND

STRETFORD END

WARWICK ROAD NORTH OLD TRAFFORD END (Away)

RAILWAY MAIN STAND

FAMILY STAND

LEICESTER CITY FC

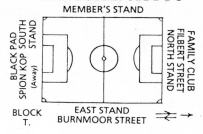

MEMBER'S STAND

BLACK PAD SPION KOP SOUTH STAND (Away)

FAMILY CLUB FILBERT STREET NORTH STAND

BLOCK T.

EAST STAND BURNMOOR STREET

LINCOLN CITY FC

SINCIL BANK (Away)

SOUTH PARK STAND

RAILWAY TERRACING

ST ANDREW'S STAND

LUTON TOWN FC

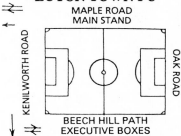

MAPLE ROAD MAIN STAND

KENILWORTH ROAD

OAK ROAD

BEECH HILL PATH EXECUTIVE BOXES

MANCHESTER CITY FC

WILMSLOW ROAD KIPPAX STREET

CLAREMONT ROAD NORTH STAND

PLATT LANE STAND (Away)

MAIN STAND MAINE ROAD

MANSFIELD TOWN FC

BISHOP STREET STAND

NORTH STAND

QUARRY LANE (Away)

WEST STAND

MIDDLESBROUGH FC

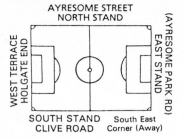

AYRESOME STREET
NORTH STAND

WEST TERRACE
HOLGATE END

(AYRESOME PARK RD)
EAST STAND

SOUTH STAND
CLIVE ROAD   South East
Corner (Away)

NEWCASTLE UNITED FC

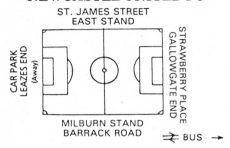

ST. JAMES STREET
EAST STAND

CAR PARK
LEAZES END
(Away)

STRAWBERRY PLACE
GALLOWGATE END

MILBURN STAND
BARRACK ROAD

BUS →

NORWICH CITY FC

SOUTH STAND

CARROW ROAD
BARCLAY STAND
(Away)
(Home)

RIVER END STAND

CITY STAND
CARROW ROAD →

NOTTS COUNTY FC

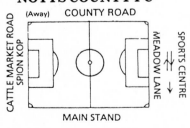

(Away)   COUNTY ROAD

CATTLE MARKET ROAD
SPION KOP

MEADOW LANE

SPORTS CENTRE

MAIN STAND

OXFORD UNITED FC

OSLER ROAD

CUCKOO LANE
(Away)

LONDON ROAD

Disabled
Section   BEECH ROAD

MILLWALL FC

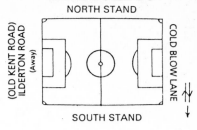

NORTH STAND

(OLD KENT ROAD)
ILDERTON ROAD
(Away)

COLD BLOW LANE

SOUTH STAND

NORTHAMPTON TOWN FC

(CRICKET PITCH SIDE) WANTAGE ROAD

SPION KOP
(Away)

HOTEL END

(Away)
ABINGDON AVENUE

NOTTINGHAM FOREST FC

EXECUTIVE STAND

RIVER TRENT
TRENT END

COLWICK ROAD
(Away)

MAIN STAND
PAVILION ROAD

OLDHAM ATHLETIC FC

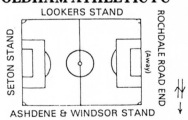

LOOKERS STAND

SETON STAND

ROCHDALE ROAD END
(Away)

ASHDENE & WINDSOR STAND

PETERBOROUGH UNITED FC

(Disabled)
GLEBE ROAD   (Stand)

MOYS END
(Away)

LONDON ROAD

Disabled
Area   MAIN STAND

MARWIN
CORNER

PLYMOUTH ARGYLE FC

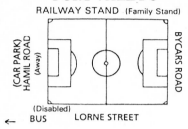

TAVISTOCK ROAD
LYNDHURST STAND

DEVONPORT END

BARN PARK
(PEVERELL) END
(Away)

GRAND STAND

PORT VALE FC

RAILWAY STAND (Family Stand)

(CAR PARK)
HAMIL ROAD
(Away)

BYCARS ROAD

(Disabled)
← BUS   LORNE STREET

QUEENS PARK RANGERS FC

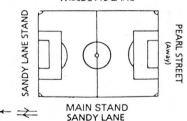

(Disabled)
ELLERSLIE ROAD STAND

LOFTUS ROAD STAND

BLOEMFONTEIN ROAD
WEST END STAND (SCHOOL)
(Away)

MAIN STAND
SOUTH AFRICA ROAD

ROCHDALE FC

WILLBUTTS LANE

SANDY LANE STAND

PEARL STREET
(Away)

MAIN STAND
SANDY LANE

SCARBOROUGH FC

CAR PARK
HINDERWELL ROAD STAND

SEAMER ROAD END

EDGEHILL ROAD
(Away)

MAIN STAND

PORTSMOUTH FC

MILTON ROAD
NORTH STAND

FROGMORE ROAD
FRATTON END

(MILTON END)
ASPLEY ROAD
(Away)

SOUTH STAND
CARISBROOKE ROAD

PRESTON NORTH END FC

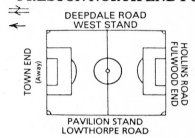

DEEPDALE ROAD
WEST STAND

TOWN END
(Away)

HOLLINS ROAD
FULWOOD END

PAVILION STAND
LOWTHORPE ROAD

READING FC

TILEHURST ROAD
(SOUTH BANK)

SUFFOLK ROAD
READING END
(Away)

WANTAGE ROAD
TILEHURST END

NORFOLK ROAD

ROTHERHAM UNITED FC

MILLMOOR LANE

MASBOROUGH STREET
TIVOLI END

RAILWAY END
(Away)

MAIN STAND

SCUNTHORPE UNITED FC

EAST STAND

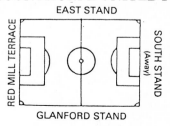

RED MILL TERRACE

SOUTH STAND
(Away)

GLANFORD STAND

101

SHEFFIELD UNITED FC

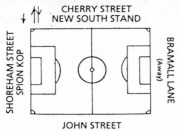

CHERRY STREET
NEW SOUTH STAND

SHOREHAM STREET
SPION KOP

BRAMALL LANE
(Away)

JOHN STREET

SHEFFIELD WEDNESDAY FC

NORTH STAND

LEPPINGS LANE
WEST STAND
(Away)

PENISTONE ROAD
SPION KOP

SOUTH STAND
RIVER DON

SHREWSBURY TOWN FC

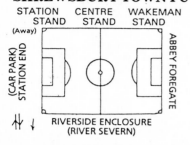

STATION STAND   CENTRE STAND   WAKEMAN STAND
(Away)

(CAR PARK)
STATION END

ABBEY FOREGATE

RIVERSIDE ENCLOSURE
(RIVER SEVERN)

SOUTHAMPTON FC

EAST STAND

ARCHERS ROAD
(Away)

WILTON AVENUE
MILTON ROAD

WEST STAND
HILL LANE/MILTON ROAD

SOUTHEND UNITED FC

SHAKESPEARE DRIVE
WEST STAND

ROOTS HALL AVE.
WEST STREET
SOUTH BANK
(Away)

FAIRFAX DRIVE
NORTH BANK

EAST STAND
VICTORIA AVENUE

STOCKPORT COUNTY FC

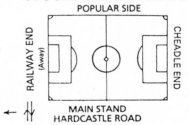

POPULAR SIDE

RAILWAY END
(Away)

CHEADLE END

MAIN STAND
HARDCASTLE ROAD

STOKE CITY FC

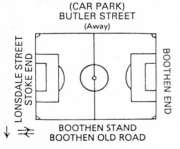

(CAR PARK)
BUTLER STREET
(Away)

LONSDALE STREET
STOKE END

BOOTHEN END

BOOTHEN STAND
BOOTHEN OLD ROAD

SUNDERLAND AFC

ASSOCIATION ROAD
CLOCK STAND

ROKER BATHS ROAD
ROKER END
(Away)

HAMPDEN ROAD
FULWELL END

ROKER WING   CENTRE STAND   FULWELL WING

SWANSEA CITY FC

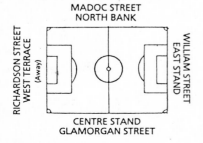

MADOC STREET
NORTH BANK

RICHARDSON STREET
WEST TERRACE
(Away)

WILLIAM STREET
EAST STAND

CENTRE STAND
GLAMORGAN STREET

SWINDON TOWN FC

NORTH STAND

COUNTY ROAD
TOWN END

STRATTON BANK
(Away)

SOUTH STAND
SHRIVENHAM ROAD

TORQUAY UNITED FC

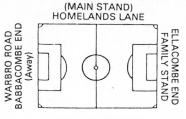

(MAIN STAND)
HOMELANDS LANE

WARBRO ROAD
BABBACOMBE END
(Away)

ELLACOMBE END
FAMILY STAND

MARNHAM ROAD
POPULAR SIDE

TOTTENHAM HOTSPUR FC

WORCESTER AVENUE
EAST STAND

PAXTON ROAD
NORTH STAND
(Members Only)

PARK LANE
SOUTH STAND
(Away)

WEST STAND
HIGH ROAD

TRANMERE ROVERS FC

CAR PARK
FAMILY ENCLOSURE MAIN STAND

BEBINGTON KOP END
(Away)

TOWN END
PRENTON ROAD WEST

BOROUGH ROAD SIDE

WALSALL FC

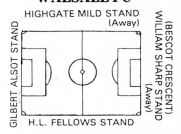

HIGHGATE MILD STAND
(Away)

GILBERT ALSOT STAND

(BESCOT CRESCENT)
WILLIAM SHARP STAND
(Away)

H.L. FELLOWS STAND

WATFORD FC

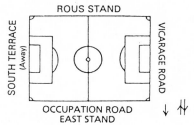

ROUS STAND

SOUTH TERRACE
(Away)

VICARAGE ROAD

OCCUPATION ROAD
EAST STAND

WEST BROMWICH ALBION FC

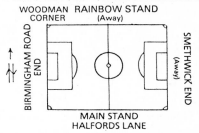

WOODMAN   RAINBOW STAND
CORNER   (Away)

BIRMINGHAM ROAD
END

SMETHWICK END
(Away)

MAIN STAND
HALFORDS LANE

WEST HAM UNITED FC

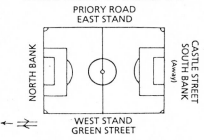

PRIORY ROAD
EAST STAND

NORTH BANK

CASTLE STREET
SOUTH BANK
(Away)

WEST STAND
GREEN STREET

WIGAN ATHLETIC FC

HEINZ
FAMILY   PHOENIX STAND
ENCLOSURE

SPRINGFIELD ROAD
TOWN END

SHEVINGTON END
(Away)

POPULAR SIDE
ST. ANDREWS DRIVE

WIMBLEDON FC

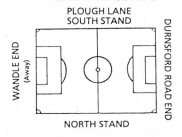

PLOUGH LANE
SOUTH STAND

WANDLE END
(Away)

DURNSFORD ROAD END

NORTH STAND

WOLVERHAMPTON WANDERERS FC

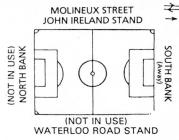

MOLINEUX STREET
JOHN IRELAND STAND

(NOT IN USE)
NORTH BANK

SOUTH BANK
(Away)

(NOT IN USE)
WATERLOO ROAD STAND

103

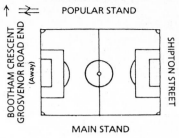

WREXHAM FC

(CAR PARK)
YALE STAND

BORDER STAND
MOLD END
(Away)

CRISPIN LANE
KOP TOWN END

MOLD ROAD STAND

YORK CITY FC

POPULAR STAND

BOOTHAM CRESCENT
GROSVENOR ROAD END
(Away)

SHIPTON STREET

MAIN STAND